Woven Words

a collection of poems and prayers
from the book 'Life Journey'
by Mary Fleeson

My journey is always just beginning.
A fresh new day,
On an old, old path.
That's the blessing,
That's where the hope blossoms
However much I wandered yesterday
I can start again tomorrow
And when all my tomorrows are used up,
I'll still have travelled
And you know what people say,
It's the Journey that counts,
Not the arriving.

I pray that God will speak loudly
And that you will hear humbly.

I pray that God will act mightily
And that you will receive graciously.

I pray that God will bless amazingly
And that you will share freely.

I pray that God will be close
And that you will walk safely.

Journey

Follow

I follow Jesus
Who is man, human, whole, impartial,
Passionate, curious
And yet also God, incarnate, creative and created,
To walk beside us.

I follow the Shepherd
Like a lamb, trusting, comforted, safe,
Held in a strength beyond my own.
Knowing that I am sought, special, precious
And enabled to be.

I follow the saints,
Those who followed Him before,
Those who died, to self, for Him,
I learn from their lives, sacrifice and wisdom.
God given.

As I follow You today Lord,
let me, Your creation
discover how to be creative.

As I follow You today Lord,
let me, Your child
begin to understand how I am precious.

As I follow You today Lord,
let me, Your new saint
learn sacrifice and wisdom.

As I follow You today Lord,
let me, Your beloved
accept love from others
and give love in return.

I follow because
I am called,
desired,
loved
and
cherished
by my Creator,
my Saviour.
Asked only
to love in return,
love others
And be loved.

Lord, help me in my unbelief,
Help my heart to accept what my mind cannot understand.
May my faith be as trusting as a bird on the wing,
as simple as the beauty of a clear summer sky,
as sure as the earth beneath my feet.
May I sense the power of creation,
embrace the sacrifice of love,
and experience Your healing in my life.
Lord, thank You for hearing my prayer.

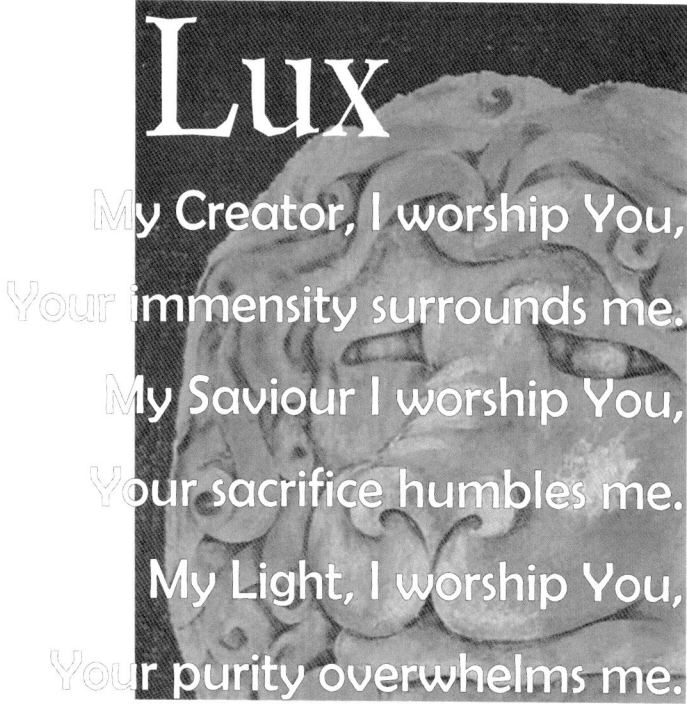

Lux

My Creator, I worship You,
Your immensity surrounds me.
My Saviour I worship You,
Your sacrifice humbles me.
My Light, I worship You,
Your purity overwhelms me.

Your breath I hear as the wind,
  whispering worship.
Your peace I seek as I travel.

Your face I see as the sun,
  smiling solace.
Your peace I seek as I travel.

Your hand I feel as the water,
  cradling comfort.
Your peace I seek as I travel.

Your

Be by my side dear Lord,
Every step I take,
Be before me, dear Lord,
Every step I take,
Be behind me dear Lord,
Every step I take,
Be in me dear Lord,
Every step I take.

Magnificat

My soul magnifies the Lord
My spirit rejoices in God my Saviour,

By grace You have given me
Life
Never ending, eternally in your presence,
Hope
Growing, maturing daily, fed by the knowledge of love,
Joy
Deep in my soul, defeating sorrow and human pain.

From before my birth You chose me
To live,
Each moment nearing fulfilment of my potential,
To worship
My Father, my Saviour, My God,
To serve
The stranger and friend in obedience and compassion.

Help me to live each moment
reaching for the fulfilment of my potential,
Help me to worship You,
my Father,
my Saviour,
my God.

Help me to serve the stranger and friend
in obedience and compassion.
I can do nothing without You
but with You I can do anything.

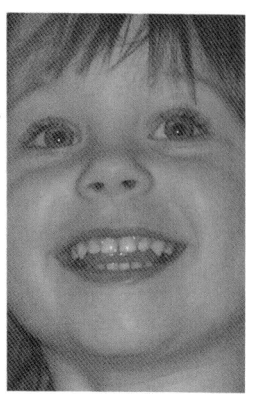

Embrace me Lord,
    As the loving parent to a new born babe,
    As the gentle wave on a windswept shore,
    As the summer breeze lifts the soaring bird,
    As the fall of rain on the parched garden soil,
    As the pure note of song caresses an ear,
    As the touch on the face from a lover,
    As the clear starlight falling on a deep, still lake,
    As the warming sunlight on a butterfly wing,
    As the brushstroke on a painter's canvas,
    As the soft hug of a much loved toy,
    As the familiar words of a memorised poem,
        Embrace me O Lord.

Touch

Here I am God,
    standing/kneeling/sitting
    before You.
Examine my heart God,
    show me Your will.
Here I am Lord,
    crying/joyful/fearful
    before You.
Reveal my need Lord,
    show me Your will.

You say that it is Your blood, shed for me,
I drink and believe in the one true God.

You say I should give to God
what belongs to Him,
I give myself and long to return home.

You say that I shouldn't judge others,
I try to see your smile on the stranger's face.

You say that if I am burdened
You will give me rest,
I am freed from the stress and the pain.

You say that I should go out to all nations,
I pray I'll be ready for your call.

You said that you would be with me always,
I am peaceful and I am secure.

Show me

**Precious Lord,
to obey you, willingly,
to love, unconditionally,
to live, kindly,
to help others, joyfully,
to praise, childishly,**

My precious Lord.

Adore the Lord your God
He loves you,
Confess your sin to Him
He forgives you,
Thank Him for His mercy
He conquered death,
Surrender your desires
He is Life.

With my mind,
my body and my spirit
I worship You Lord,
Help me to love You more.

I'm sorry
I have made You sad,
so many times.
Help me to do Your will.

With my mind,
my body and my spirit
I thank You Lord,
Without You I am nothing.

I'm offering You
my hopes
and my dreams,
Help me to share Your wisdom.

Creator God,
never ending,
eternal,
perfect,
Circle me.
Merciful God,
protect and save
all those I love
Circle me.
Awesome God,
restore me
and keep me safe
Circle me.

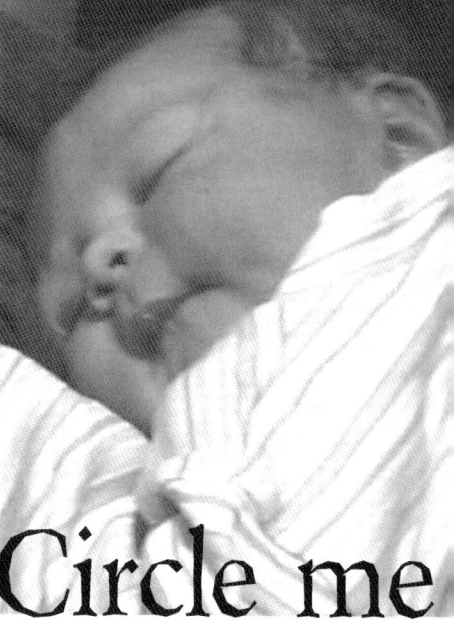

Circle me

Circle me Lord, let love be my reason,
Let hate be a stranger.
Circle me Lord, let joy be my comfort,
Let sadness be no more.
Circle me Lord, let peace be my aim,
Let conflict be resolved.
Circle me Lord, let love be my reason,
Let hate be a stranger.
Circle me Lord, let joy be my comfort,
Let sadness be no more.
Circle me Lord, let peace be my aim,
Let conflict be resolved.

If I were Eve in the Garden of Eden
Would I be taken in by a talking snake?
If I were Adam in that Paradise place
Would I risk it all for my partner's sake?
If I were a leader on this garden planet
Would I hear the word 'kill' and obey?
If I were alone, my people all lost
Would I fall to my knees and pray?
If I were living in a land where 'a' hated 'b'
Would I follow the crowd or stop to ask why?
If I were to offer my friendship to another
Would they turn their back or smile and cry?

Tree

Healing Lord,

Open the hearts
of those in conflict,
help them to receive
your healing.
Merciful Lord,
May our human hearts
never harden
to the suffering caused by
the absence of peace,
help us to yearn for peace.
Almighty Lord,
Help us to see where we are
avoiding reconciliation,
please grant us opportunities
and the will to change.

Strong and awesome Father,
sacrificial and wise Son,
supporting and restoring Spirit,
Hear my prayer.

I am small, such a little creature and yet
I believe that You know me.
I believe that You created me,
I believe that You wanted me to be part of Your world.
I believe that I have a place, a purpose, in Your world,

When that place and purpose
is hidden from my sight
please grant me patience
and perseverance.

Don't let me go.

Strong and awesome Father,
sacrificial and wise Son,
supporting and restoring Spirit,
Hear my prayer.

Grace

Graceful Trinity of love,
Hear our prayer.
You were at the beginning,
You are now,
You shall be evermore.
Grant us peace.
With the ebb of the tide,
With the turn of the season,
Grant us peace.
Father, Son and Spirit,
Hear our prayer.

Heart

A pain, deeply buried
(deep cries out to deep),
Our innermost core of being
(He knows the emptiness),
Cracked, torn and barren
(He longs to fill),
Only our vulnerability
(To God and to each other),
Will allow to heal
(He wants to heal you),
His desire is to soothe and protect
(For this He died).

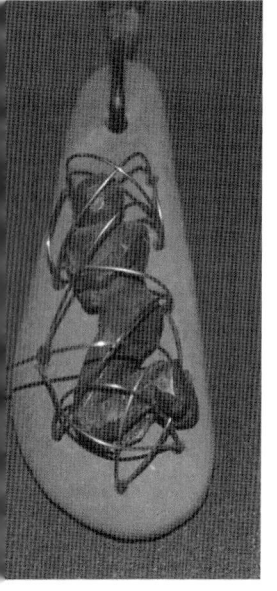

When all seems black,
help me to remember
the peace of Your promise,

When all seems dark,
help me to remember
the purity of Your light,

When all seems hopeless,
help me to remember
the comfort of Your words,

When all seems discord,
help me to remember
the harmony of Your creation.

Life Journey

May my conversations be significant,
May my meetings be blessed,
May my path cross the paths
of others who love You.
May my path cross the paths
of others who don't know You.
May my touch
be Your touch
of infinite gentleness,
May my words
be Your words
of wisdom,
May my eyes see
with Your compassion.

Life journey
winding,
Patterns
undulating,
overlapping
Weaving
community.
Touch
as you pass,
smile,
hold the
moment
As God
holds you
in His heart.

Copyright © 2017 by Mary and Mark Fleeson.
This edition copyright © 2017 Lindisfarne Scriptorium Limited.

The authors reserve the moral right to be identified as the authors of this work.

 This edition published by: Lindisfarne Scriptorium Limited, Farne House, Marygate, Holy Island of Lindisfarne, TD15 2SJ United Kingdom. www.lindisfarne-scriptorium.co.uk

ISBN-13: 978 1 909041 23 3

10 9 8 7 6 5 4 3 2 1

British Library Cataloguing in Publication Data. A catalogue record for this book is available from the British Library.
Typeset by Lindisfarne Scriptorium Limited.
Book production and preparation by Burning Light Solutions Limited.